MW01132699

An Archeology
of the Future

An Archeology
of the Future

Emma Catherine Hoff

Children's Art Foundation–Stone Soup Inc.
Santa Cruz, California

Book design by Jeff Piekarz
Typeset in Quincy and Neue Haas Unica

ISBN: 978-0-89409-155-1 (hardcover)

Library of Congress Control Number: 2023939554

www.stonesoup.com

Printed in the United States of America

First edition

Cover: *The Little Mermaid* by Rebecca Wu, 9 (WA)
Originally appeared in the January 2021 issue of *Stone Soup*

TABLE OF CONTENTS

The graffiti of the poor is under the earth.
— Tomaž Šalamun

THE LAMP

The light shines innocently,
but it blinds me,
my eyes become red.

I shy from it
and still it follows me
with its intense gaze
boring into me as I walk around the room.

I feel the hot bulb,
sense the lamp melting
and perspiring under its own fever,
its own light.

The business is done,
I think,
but my dreams that night are of
that still figure creeping up on me,
and the next day, I find the lamp
standing again.

It glares at me
and whispers in my ear,
burning it, telling me
that the sun's light is not enough.

I ask it how it knows,
but the sun dies
and the lamp is still glowing
and I am grateful for it now.

We make our way through the darkness
until it parts with me,
saying it must go,
its filament cannot take
the strain anymore

and that the darkness isn't as bad
as people think.

WE ARE SAFER WHEN WE ARE HIDDEN

From caverns of blue,
a cloud of white is released,
and in that cloud, a shape is hiding, kicking
its legs out, propelling the storm.

Everything pours out of it at once:
rain, snow, the jump of a frog, the hoot
of an owl, the many sweaters knitted
from the fur that litters the trails
of the forest.

Whoever followed those darkening paths
armed with two knitting needles was either
a devoted tailor or a proud grandmother,
becoming the wolf that is inside,
howling for all to hear, ignoring the
gunshots that ring out, heading back
into civilization as dawn nears.

The running river makes an endless weeping
noise, restrained, as if something were
pinching it by the nose, but the world,
the thing of things, still hiding in all the corners
of itself, is happy with the life it has created.

And the game continues, the universe
a ceaseless collage of color, the words mushed
together, our planet pleading with the other planets,
so many people floating through space,
from place to place, the celestial debt
paid with crumbling rock and dead leaves.

People will think, *Soon it will be me,*
and neglect their chores,
we will all wait, the world will stop working,
We live for ourselves and ourselves only.

HOW DO I SAY REGRET?

I regret
that the dead mosquito's
legs were tied in a knot,
and no one had cared to clean it up.

I regret
that loaves of bread
are forced to rise in the oven,
with burning cheeks and begging mouths.

I regret
that things fall apart
and never come together
in a wind of bolts and pieces.

Collapse,
everything that has been standing for so long!
You are not important
and did not ever hold our hearts.

We stare at your broken parts
and set our mouths in lines
and say things that are only sometimes said.
We speak the words of people in denial.

I am sorry
for the things that never got to have a funeral
and were pushed aside
as dust that had finished falling.

I am sorry
for the journeys that had to end in one place,
your feet stomping through the jungles
and the lakes that you wanted to go to.

I am sorry
for the cushions that have been
fluffed and squished so many times,
letting all your air out.

Things that are not there
compete with you for space
and become your prison,
closing you in.

I ask for forgiveness
from the orchid,
which meant a lot to my father,
but to itself, too,

for flowers are vain
and grow such beautiful petals,
which eventually
fall off.

I ask for forgiveness
from the many coats I've worn,
tossed aside every evening
after the snow.

I ask for forgiveness
from the words that cried
so many times over mispronunciations,
sizzling like fried potatoes,

words angry about being used
in vocabulary lessons,
scratched out in pencil on worksheets,
and my asking, how do I say this?

ON AN EQUESTRIAN FARM [1]

Here I am.
Granting you the vision of the wooden chair
that we brought from the first living room
because we didn't have enough chairs for the dining room.
You see the fake flowers, they will never live real lives, never die.
They will never smell like honey, never wilt.
They must always watch us,
the humans, do the tedious things we do.
The sliding door. With the bug screen.
Yesterday night we went through that door.
Out on the porch, we petted Trevor, who was not our cat.
We don't own the farm, we don't work on it.
We won't stay at the house. Soon, it will be all alone again.
And there will be no footsteps on the staircase.
And the painted china will no longer rattle
until the next people come.
And there is a little footstool
with its broken back. With a mahogany top.
Polished wood bottom. We do not get splinters on the floorboards.
They have been washed, sanded, many times. We see a little cart.
Also made of wood, oh pretty wood, and carved in ways that I couldn't
carve. I cannot carve. The ladder in the back moves up and down,
the horse has run away, tired of carrying your load of goods.
Outside, bright sun, grass to run on,
marsh where you can sink, sneakers and all.
The horses, they were angry,
or they just wanted to scream, neigh, "Someone, come!"
And Trevor, ears perked up, hissed at a bird that was too loud,
    too happy.
And yet, Trevor did not move from his place on the porch.
He just glared like a madman and settled down, ready to be petted
some more. And my mother lounged in a chair,
and my father had gone inside with his camera, only to come out again.
And the flies were dancing and buzzing, and joining in,
and there was some sort of silent party with no music,
because the only sounds were the birds and we wanted that.

We never wanted it to stop, just wanted to stay, my mother and father with
their wine, laughing, me, running, slipping in the wet grass, laughing at the chickens.
The chicken that came up the steps with its loud claws,
the chicken that greeted me with the call of its throat,
the chicken I shied from,
the chicken with menacing eyes,
and yet Trevor's yellow eyes were more menacing.
And the barn held nothing but chickens and horses,
and the occasional cat, of which there were three.
Two cats would not greet us, were not friendly.
One ran into the bushes, another stayed on the porch, back arched.
The calico, and the tuxedo.
We don't have names for those yet.
They are not ours, do not want to be ours.
We have no ocean in front of our house, yet all of the paintings on
the walls are farms, farms with oceans stretching, waking from deep sleeps.
Our house, the house that is not really ours, has a dirt road in front of it.
No, gravel. We have no forest either.
No boat approaching the forest.
Why do the paintings lie?
Are these real places, or are they just what someone wants to see?
One of the chairs has vines engulfing it,
yet the vines are just patterns. You cannot feel them. They are not real.
There are many doors
in the house. And so many closets, with locks that are rusted shut.
One closet opened and had a light with a chain so you could turn it on,
and a staircase, which led to a ceiling on which you could bump
your head. There is nothing to walk towards.
And there is a rug in the second living room,
which has pretty flower patterns on it,
on which you can roll and become the flowers.
These flowers aren't trying hard, don't have bright pink colors.
These flowers are brown, perfect.

FOR TOMAŽ ŠALAMUN ON A RAINY DAY

The sleepers awoke,
and the wakers fell into bed.
The pens stopped,
and the sloshing of wheels in rain increased
and quieted until the only sounds
that could be heard were the senses
overwhelmed by the
tremor of the window
and the frantic waving of the trees.

People fell in the streets.

The warmth grew cold,
and the cold flew to Florida,
the plants shuddered
and the snow closed its eyes,
the walls of old houses had visions,
all the planes traveled to where you were born,
so that you could run back to your Maruska and wave,
slowly and carefully, a blurry figure.
Keys stopped tapping,
but only for a moment,
couch cushions lay alone,
ovens stood ignored.

People slept in the streets.

Forbidden words were said,
and manners were locked in boxes,
children's toys were hammered to pieces,
crayons melted under the sun,
dolls' hair was snipped until the soft scalps were bare,
strange contraptions were invented,
traveling through time was attempted,
teachers tried to gain the attention of sleeping classes,
furniture was left out to be soaked in the streets,

refrigerators sat empty and unopened,
boxes stared at each other with darkened eyes,
they knew that you had made your journey
with hair still on your head, not completely white.

People laughed in the streets.

The ants crept quietly over the lions,
and the lions tiptoed over anthills,
crab apples lay unaccepted by nature,
mulberries were cradled in careful hands,
the sidewalks became streaked with puddles
and the birds flew for cover, skidding over
people's heads and into the ivy,
kings and queens remained sheltered in their castles
with tall walls and iron gates that creaked on their hinges,
storybooks opened, then closed,
as people thought of you, the wooden questioner,
hovering over the hills of stone.

People wept in the streets.

Poetry was read,
lines were muttered,
rhymes were said,
times were uttered,
and feet tread
where deep messages led,
away from home,
away from life.

KIDS, GET YOUR MACHETES

We looked towards Arizona
                                and saw the desert
and cringed,
                letting something shake our limbs,
                                        puffing out our chests,
        it was already hot in the boiling car that huffed,
its engine stirring,
                                and disappeared, never existing, turning
                                our clothes to shreds
as we plonked on the burning sand
                                        and pricked our fingers
on cactuses.

We sailed to Cuba,
                and felt like we were seeing what we weren't supposed to see,
                        shrugging our shoulders
and dipping our hands into the cool water,
                                        but it was too late—
you have a stub of a finger and I fell all the way in—do you miss me
                        as I sit in the hollow of a shark's stomach?

We walked to the North Pole
                        without any jackets
or shirts or clothes
                and asked for warm cider or any type of drink at the bar,
                                and they told me I was too young
and that you were too old, and that we weren't wearing anything
                (we already knew that)
                        and that on Santa's orders there was only milk
and cookies at the counter.
                        "Kids, get your machetes, there's no beer here!"

We jumped to Mexico,
                        scowling and asking about where we were,
because we didn't know ourselves,
                        and then we asked who we were

and everyone averted their eyes
                              because they didn't know the answer
and we didn't either,
                    it was a hard question.

We slithered to the Pacific Ocean,
                              our skin blistering and burning
from the thought of the deserts we had crossed,
                              and fell to the sharks yet again.
I was a sort of ghost, adventurous, playing with my own pain,
                              and then the eel stung me and my
leg evaporated
    and a walrus from Nowhere prodded my arm and that was gone too,
and you were also gone,
                        and I rode on the back of a stingray
and let the rest of myself disappear.

TO YOU I GRANT MY BODY

1

My arms,
limbs connected to my body
by strips of bone and skin,
I shake my body vigorously,
my hair flies
in all directions,
my throat pulsates,
my wrist spasms,
my arms,
slowly they disconnect
and leave me.

2

Legs
oh, many walks I have taken
with my legs,
an extra thumb,
lengthening my body
taking from it
shape and size,
we were all born with legs,
but they were small ones,
useless,
useless forever,
take them,
for I thrust them into
the arms of the tree,
if the tree has arms
and it absorbs them,
becoming a peculiar color
but taller,
reaching to the sky,
never looking back
towards the ground.

3

Little bony fingers,
fragile knuckles,
I need not be a breakable
vase anymore.
I light a match,
deep inside the folds of my skin,
underneath my little
broken nails,
and my fingers shoot
off towards
space
to orbit Saturn
and join its rings.

4

Eyes,
constantly blinking,
I give them to the blind coward
who hides,
curled up in a ball
like a hedgehog,
from society,
whimpering
and cowering,
begging
to see,
to open his enclosure,
his castle,
his barrier.

5

Lips,
oh, precious lips,
if you happened to be
ripped off,
my teeth and gums
would be exposed,
my face would be pearly
white but
bloody,
the woman with the dentures
wants lips
to contain her clacking,
her lipless face
is asking for a prize,
a treasure,
something to wear on a special
occasion.
I grant this gift.

6

Torso,
rolling around
by itself on the ground,
for the biggest foot
to kick it like a soccer
ball and run.
This haunted piece
of body
cannot be destroyed.
So hard,
so big,
it breaks every little bone
in the foot.
Gift your foot back
to me,
for that is the thing I am missing.

ON AN EQUESTRIAN FARM [2]

There was a day on the farm that was not like the others.
Because the orange cat (we named her Claire) had finally come up to us,
and she was ready to flirt with us. She meowed at us, begged us for attention with
mischievous eyes, but when we tried to pet her,
oh, the sight! She scurried away as if we were hurting her.
She told us she thought our hands were dirty, and if we were a self-conscious family
we would have looked at our hands,
and we would have run inside and washed them and glared at the cat out the window,
who would be licking herself like nothing had happened.
This was the day that we learned a funny thing, that Trevor was a girl
and that Claire and the black-and-white cat (Patricia, Pat for short)
were boys, through and through. And yet, as we learned their real names, we
forgot them all the same, and the only cat's name we could remember was Trevor's.
Trevor's name was Fern, and my parents called her that,
but I was so used to Trevor that I continued to mix up the cats,
girl for boy, boy for girl.
And then we met another miracle! A miracle that only nature herself could have given us.
Another cat, who did not belong to the people on the farm
but came and ate all the food anyway.
And this cat's name was a name that I remembered:
Lint. Like the stuff that sticks to clothes. This cat stuck to the farm,
with its grassy hills and beautiful skies, and the high grass that my dad led my
mom and me into, despite my warnings of tick territory
(it did turn out to be tick territory),
and so we squelched through mud, only to find that the forest did not have a trail,
as my dad had hoped, so we squelched back to the house,
and we took showers and glared at my dad. And onwards our adventures

stretched throughout the week we stayed, so many I cannot tell you
    about all of
them, and they were too perfect and beautiful to be written down in
    words anyway,
and it will exhaust me to tell the tale out loud,
so I am content the way things are. I know nobody likes cliffhangers.
But hold onto the cliff and climb up onto it
and you will see the farm, and everything we did there.

IT ALL ADDS UP TO FUN TIMES

Look for the hidden cracks inside the mountains.
Walk far to become your background.
Pick one of the many options that dangle before your eyes.

Tell no one of your secret benefactor.
If a traveler comes, sing your song, notes running along the river.
Hear the ripples in the water that stands still along the side
of the mountain.

See the fields, come home, for you have gone too far.
Tell me of the sheep, for you have become a pinprick in the distance.
Come towards my voice, be drawn to me.
You and me, we know of the danger.
Know, too, that you must know.

Go back into town, say hello to a few people.
Clip clop along like you are a horse, play your counting game.
Find the pretty bird.
Pay attention to the bell ringing, fly away.

You come to a fork in the road, where is the spoon?
The fortune teller says you are the knife.
Pull yourself up by your skinny jeans.
Run along: the future calls.

I cannot walk anymore in darkness, but you are not light.
We don't know anything, we do not use cotton balls
for our floor plans. We're walking through a haunted house,
so now we'll stop, drop, and roll. It all adds up to fun times.

Find me, look for me, listen to me, sit with me.
The bench is for two until someone proves it has room for three.

Remember my words, frown, smile.
Clear your face of everything, now open your eyes wide.
I will read you like a book.

PALM READING

1

Your palm facing up,
your leaf-strings, your interlocking veins,
are read.

2

Your tendrils reach down towards me,
I turn away,
your cries are heard
vibrating through your roots.

3

You keep growing,
you keep growing!
I laugh.

4

Do you constantly need water
or do you beg for the sake of begging?

5

I see the dead plants,
but you have not shriveled yet,
you reach your beautiful hand
out to me, but I am scared
to take it.

6

You play with me,
you giggle in your

watery voice,
you have no entertainment
other than me.

7

I pull something away
to see something else,
and I pull down the blinds
just as quickly,
some things are
too good to be true.

8

Words come from one mouth:
you're beautiful—
but you do not grow flowers,
you will not,
you are cruel.

9

You hide in the dirt
until I come near,
and when I do,
you watch me
as you would a clown.

10

Maybe I will find you again,
in a florist's shop, perhaps,
but that would be cliché
after all we've gone through,
maybe you will shake my
rough hand with your
soft one and say,

I have to go.

11

Asking you why
is no use:
I cannot come home,
because that is what I did
the first time:
I cannot step over the threshold
again.

PEARS

Covered whole: marigold, lime, clear untainted seagrass.
Juicy insides with crunchy wind-made skins.
The colors continue in a straight line, which is what makes the fruit
    special.
It is not blended so much as completed.

The palette itself is the art, and it can be made up of many colors,
but it is confusing.
The white highlights blink. The ropes tighten and bind.
There are multiple colors.

No. It is the lighting.
The colors are blended and are therefore one.
Spread across the entire body,
they are as true as the breaths you take.

Pick the colors apart with your fishy instruments,
you cannot blend or smash them together
any more than they already are.

SIX VISIONS OF THE END OF THE WORLD

1

Where dusty seeds flew on the wind,
and the trapped birds screamed,
scattering all the spindly-legged beings.
Where inside a boy was dividing
halves of bodies,
bird or human, it didn't matter.

2

Where there was peace
and quiet, too.
Where there were notes that floated
through the air.
Where there was silence
in the decomposing rib cages of
tigers who had tried to leap
over mountains into space.

3

Where waves lapped at the toes of unsuspecting
children playing in the sand,
chasing after seagulls.
Where there were squalls of locusts that iced the fields
and made them reach with dead and brittle fingers.

4

Where no one could speak,
for clouds the size of grapes fogged up their mouths
and stuck their teeth together.
Where children crashed their way through
trees, laughing, until they realized
there wasn't a way out.

5

Where the sky rains down daily,
and people spend their last dollars rebuilding houses
only to find their embroidered cushions buried
in the dirt.
Where batteries run down
in the electronic workings of the world
and the stars were turned inside out.

6

Where the world finally achieved nothing.
Where no one took or stole
or rolled around like a madman in a prison cell.
Where there was peace for Earth
with no one there.
Where, if you were still alive,
you could grab Saturn's rings
and they would burn you,
pull away,
and laugh.

ON A PAINTING BY HENRI ROUSSEAU

In the savanna a tiger prowls,
but once tamed it can't ever regain its power.
It will sit behind the man,
whose eyes will be glued to his paper,
his blank paper with no writing,
because his hand does not move.

A child will stand there for eternity,
not growing,
eyeing the man and his tiger,
with a puppet,
which she wanted to bring to her special spot
that is taken forever,
her flower crown dangling in sadness,
unable to take another step.

If the hot sun beats down,
the motionless people will not feel it.
If its rays blind them,
they will be blinded like they already are.

The plants should grow or wilt, but they do neither.
They have decided on their size,
they have decided to be immortal,
to not move,
to not dangle,
to not fall.

If there is no wind, the hot-air balloons are not floating.
If there is wind, it is not real,
in an already unreal clear blue sky.
The animals?
They just stare,
and even that they don't do.

If you touched the lion, it would not roar,
if you write something it will vanish,
if you take a step you're stuck.
Everything is frozen yet moving.

AN ELEGY FOR BOBBY HUTTON

I think you missed
the birds calling in those last moments.

I think the leaves
stopped rustling
when the bullets hit.

I wish you were able
to hear
the trees whisper
and the flowers grow
instead of the guns
and the creaking of
the burning house.

I think you missed
how every single pair
of paws was clasped together
in prayer for you.

I think you missed it
while you were falling.

I think you missed
how the mud
parted ways for you.

I think you missed
your own funeral
but doesn't everyone?

You were entangled
in black shadows,
you were pulled farther
back, you were pulled inside.

I think
you didn't see the tears
because you
couldn't cry.

I know
your eyes were closed.

Can I take it for granted
that your limbs were straight,
or were they slowly
breaking in that casket?

Did you know what
happened afterwards,
or was your head
just blank forevermore?

I don't think
you saw the way
the others mourned.

You were far,
far away,
maybe even nowhere.

THREE THINGS THAT WERE RECENTLY FOUND
FLOATING IN THE SKY

Eye

And in the midst of the moon, the eye was squinting. The eye had a dare for you: take off your shoes and hail a ride on the cold air. Freeze your feet into dust and see if the moon can repair them again. The moon is made of rock, not cheese, there is no man living inside it, it's petrified, and it has no knowledge that was supposedly gotten from the books in the Harvard library.

Blush

The sun's blush was made of flames. Flames that rained from the second sky, which the sun then bought at the farmer's market in cautiously harvested clumps. The sun applies this blush daily, and it is so strong, that we look up and we see the sun striding on an asteroid belt catwalk, glimmering like ages of glass put together in a mosaic. Sometimes, there are eclipses. That's when the sun has to sign too many autographs.

Lips

When the lips whispered, they only whispered important secrets. Mercury's messenger speaking to Pluto, and back again, traveling on light-years and beams. The lips play leapfrog with rain and hail and snow and command the clouds to move and command the sky to reform every day after the moon takes over. There are constant revolts in the galaxy, and the lips are the reason.

DEAR FRIEND

They are dressed as if they just went to a funeral.
Which they did.
But only I know.

They went to mourn
in Los Angeles,
and are staying at a hotel now.
They are probably taking off
dresses and ties.

They're coming home tomorrow.
I begged to go,
but Mom asked me what funeral I was talking about.

Yesterday
I got a letter.
It said,

"Dear friend,
We miss you.
We are coming home soon.
The funeral was sad.
Wish you could be there.
Love,
Your friends."

Today
my friends
came back.

While I helped them
Take off their coats,
one of them asked,
"Did you get our letter?"

I felt happy
even though the handwriting on the letter
was mine.

PEOPLE YOU MAY SOMEDAY MEET

I've met the man on the corner in the hat who yells at everybody, but
I never shook hands with him or understood anything he said,
which is sad, because if no one understands what you say, then
your language hardly exists.

I've met the lady I saw at a public garden who seemed right out of a
comedy because she would talk about the most random things
and then keep going on about something else like she was
incapable of stopping.

I've seen the guy who walks his dog sometimes in the middle of
winter in a Hawaiian shirt, cargo shorts, and flip-flops. But I've
never seen him in summer. Maybe he's frozen into a block of ice
and hasn't melted yet.

I've met the guy who sits under his living room window on the
sidewalk in a beach chair and smokes a cigarette while reading a
magazine when it's cold, and the smoke is a kind of wave or "hello"
for me, but when it's warm, he moves his chair underneath the
wooden post that seems to balance all the clouds on the sidewalk.

I've met the doorman who I always say "hi" to when I leave the
building, to which he says "bye," and even though he's very nice
it's always awkward.

I've met the man who works at the Broad museum of contemporary
art, who let us in and stared right at me really intensely as he
talked about not touching the artwork.

I've met the daydream of you, Tomaž, the poet I wanted to meet,
though you died before I could even read.

I've met the lunch aide that everybody thought was mean but was
actually very nice: she had a bad elbow or something.

I've met the rumors of a strict teacher who I might have this year, and
then again, I've met another teacher who people said the same
things about. Maybe one of them would like this poem.

I've met the man who fixed a ring that was too big for my mom's
finger, and now it's tight but also loose in a good way, like one of
these lines could wrap around someone I've met.

IRONY

"You can climb up
the rope," said Sarah
to Lucy.
And she almost wanted
it to be true because she
meant to say, "I won't be
able to stand it if you fall
off again."

Johnny thought he could
get straight As
if he pretended
to be listening while
he was really drawing
his teacher,
but he was caught
after a whole month
of him acting
and was told that report
cards wouldn't be given out in a while
and that he should give up his
whole charade.

Belle's fish was going
to die, and she didn't
want her mother to get
rid of it by flushing it
down the toilet,
but the fish died while
Belle was in school,
and Belle's mother
couldn't stand looking
at its dead body,
so she disposed of it
and got a new fish
which she claimed was

Belle's perfectly healthy
"old fish."

Belle never guessed
and neither would Johnny
have if he hadn't been told.

And Lucy fell off
the rope and Sarah ran outside
and cried.

And Sarah read this very
poem and thought about Lucy,
and Lucy read it and thought about Sarah,
and Belle finally guessed
what she would never have
guessed and Johnny remembered.

And Belle's new fish
swam around until it,
too,
died, but Belle was
guarding it with a pitchfork.

And this poem unraveled
like a ball of yarn
and stuck to Johnny's cheek
and made him sulk.

And Lucy pretended to
hug Sarah but slapped
her instead, and Sarah
did some more crying.

And the rope in the gym
hung depressed and sad
and decided that it would
never be climbed again,

and Johnny's drawings
of the teacher were found
by Sarah, who gave them
to Belle, who gave them
to Lucy, who gave them to
the unclimbable
rope, covered in
post-it notes
and protecting every
last line of poetry
that comedy concocted.

71 FACES

We looked at the pistachio's face,
the face of the smoke from the chimneys,
and the faces of green leaves.
The face of the vase broken apart for the fifteenth time,
and the faces of the roses withered without water.
The pillow face upon which we pick strawberries,
the couch face, complaining.
The human in the wall face,
such a white face, white enough to blend in with the white wall.
You can see the faces of the veins through the faces of the pale hands.
Oh, look, there is Kenneth Koch's face,
lemon-shaped glasses, big-eared countenance, open mouth talking,
    talking.
The split-open spider face, a face with a bushy mustache,
the detective face wearing a deerstalker cap.

The goodbye face,
the I'm back face.
The interesting face perched upon the bird face,
perched upon the moon face,
the half face, the full face, the crescent face, the gibbous face.
The face of war and blood on dirt,
the smiling face, the shocked face,
the face in the outlet,
the face of death.
The faces of those in the tanks and of those in houses,
and of those pulling levers or giving orders,
the faces of those that are nowhere.
The faces of those that have lost buttons
and the faces of those that have lost relatives, spouses, children, and
    friends.

The jacket face has a tongue like a zipper poking out at me.
The history face and the current events face that will eventually be
    a history face.
The comma face yelling at the apostrophe face.

The knock-knock joke face yelling at the dad joke face
and zero telling eight that it has a nice belt.
The chatting before a test face
and the poisonous flower face that makes you put on a frowny face
and your safe-at-home-until-you're-not face.
And just a regular blank face that is never blank because it is a face.
There is the pen face and the poet's face,
and there is the Greek god face and the Bible face for all you religious
    faces,
and here's the face full of roots and the face full of earth.
There's the culture face that wants to rub its culture everywhere.
The bit-by-bit face, the pixelated face, the things are falling apart
    face.

I see the dead face and the dying face with the cigarette still in its
    mouth.
I see the face that won't give up and the pleading face and the crying
    face and the questioning face.
I see the paperclip face, puncturing everything.
I want to make the uncushioned-white-clean-chair-in-the-laundry-
    room-that-is-very-hard face a thing again.
I want to make the face of a cold cycle and a warm cycle and a wet
    cycle.
I want to find the face of the birdlike open door.
I want to make this a face.
I want to count every face that is a face.

YOUR QUESTION IS A FOOL

Asking for a pen to write himself down with—
pursuing a long, twisting road, and asking,
Who must I be? He continues to look for examples,
prompts, and meaning, insisting that he cannot
retreat into the shell of a body before he has answers.

We cannot give you answers, we protest,
and it is as if we are bargaining, except he knows what we will tell him,
No, and so he keeps lowering the price—
we refuse, for we are not bestowed with knowledge about others,
only about ourselves.

We are human, are we not?
And yet he says that we are animals,
growling and pawing at the ground,
afraid in a cage.

And so, we part with him, indignant,
and he is left on his own, the bellowing elephant,
the screeching crow,
begging the trees, the sacred elms,
the legendary seers, for the answers we did not give him.

But even the hearty bark gives no signs,
nor do the wise leaves at all rustle,
they simply stare at him mournfully as he walks away,
wondering, *What is wrong with me?*

A chill ripples through him as he is tossed to the waves and the void.
Do you know? he pleads. *Do you know?*
Yes, whispers the water. *No,* adds the world.
All together, they sing, *Your question is a fool.*

PLAYTIME

The chipmunk scurries
along branches, notes played by hands
that held onto the keys for so long,
until everything broke off,
until the music broke off and the little chipmunk stopped scurrying.

The bird has a tree that fell down,
and it takes into the air,
while the squirrels, clever acrobats,
sneaky tricksters,
jump from branch to branch when the thin limb starts
to waver.

The little chipmunk does not control
this quaver and instead
falls, down, down, onto the road.
If he's lucky, he will fall into mud,
but it did not rain last night,
it was only windy.

Shush,
little chipmunk,
shush your cries.
I saw you on the forest path,
I never thought you'd die,
and here you are,
motionless, lying like those baby birds.
I can imagine you, falling apart,
the walls of your body washed away,
like that fairy house my dad and I made
and placed in the forest.

Nothing lasts on a windy day,
and then comes rain,
and nothing lasts on a rainy day,
and the branches that did last

glisten with water and dew,
rocking in the wind.

HOW TO SHARE AN APRICOT

I shared
my apricot
with a bird.

It said,
"Thank you."
I don't know when the bird started talking.

It wrapped me in its arms.
It had a gentle grip.
Such a gentle grip.
Too gentle of a grip, I thought.
Supernatural.

I don't know
when the bird grew arms.

All I know
are my thoughts.
Right then I was thinking this was not a good way to show gratitude.

I didn't know
where it was taking me.

But then the bird vanished.
Its gentle grip was gone.
And I was falling.

I landed
in a queer place.
Above me
stood a human with a beak.

And I knew at once
that it was Carry,
the animal I shared my apricot with.

All I could think was the
sweet, sweet fact
that above me there were several apricots.

And I wanted to have one,
for I had shared mine earlier today
with a bird.

THE AMBASSADOR

after de Chirico

An ambassador.
He has no mind, no face.
He sits back in a daze.

Like a dog,
loyal
to anyone who commands him to do anything.
But with no mind.

No, he stoops lower than a dog.
He is not human anymore.
He wears a breastplate—
for every moment he is ready for a battle to lose.

People treat him like a toy,
a robot.
Yet there are no people.

Where he sits is not a city,
but it has walls.
It has no hope,
yet it has strength.
Perhaps the walls have hope, the ambassador thinks.

The walls could talk.
Or could they?
They talked to him.

He knows he is nothing.
He wants to give himself away.
Leave the curtain and chair, and enter the darkness beyond,
where he will have to suffer nothing.
But then the walls would be alone.

Does he already suffer nothing?
He is alive and not alive.
How does he think?
He is alive and not alive.

Like a tree
he stands still, not quite able to grasp the knife
that he could put to his breastplate
to ruin the mechanisms that hide there.
To be gone
from an awful world he is already gone from.

A PANTOUM OF THE NEW WORLD

Long nights away from home,
coming to the lands where they play,
I will fight until I reach my tomb,
at least that's what they say.

Coming to the lands where they play,
where their chatter is for sale,
at least that's what they say,
nobody's home, the day is pale.

Where their chatter is for sale,
colonizers knock and knock,
nobody's home the day is pale,
and yet, upon the grass falls the lock.

Colonizers knock and knock,
then they gather around the fire,
and yet, upon the grass falls the lock,
they brag their swords will never tire.

Then they gather around the fire,
mighty feet stamping the ashes on the ground,
they brag their swords will never tire,
their horses will never stop being loud.

Mighty feet stamping the ashes on the ground,
I am a conquistador, and you, a pilgrim,
their horses will never stop being loud,
Listen to me, let's make a deal.

I am a conquistador and you are a pilgrim,
I'm out of town one day and back the next,
listen to me, let's make a deal,
we will live on as heroes.

I'm out of town one day and back the next,
I will fight until I reach my tomb,
they live on as monsters,
long nights away from home.

ON A PHOTOGRAPH BY PEDRO LUIS RAOTA

The early death of the man behind the camera propels him
to make everything live forever, for it all to be old,
like the woman, barely looked at by anyone.
And as the soldiers pass by, their guns heavy on their shoulders,
the scene is immortalized in shadows and darkness.
At home, he blurs the figures angrily, but they're still
marching through the streets,

and the woman is somewhere else now, kneeling on the ground.
Nobody looks at her, except the photographer,
and he only has his camera, what good will that do her?
Just a man who finds her interesting, but has nothing to offer
other than her picture.

Still, the photograph finds its way onto the wall,
framed but then destroyed by what we will never know,
and still the gray wall persists, people striding past it,
the woman still there, the photographer gone,
and suddenly, all the world had ever known was erased,
and new things came quickly and startled the people.
No longer would pictures be taken, they all declared.

AN INTERESTING AND RATHER ANNOYING ARRAY OF MONSTERS

This one took a shape of shadowy fear and molded it into the sharp
teeth of an angry hound.
This one crumpled into a corner and hid in the overactive imaginations
of sleeping children.
And this one flew with bird wings over skies and resents its talons.

This one haunted you and your walls and likes to bite.
This one hides in your pipes and scares the mice.
And this one flew with bird wings over skies and resents its talons.

This one has been noticed taking bites of bridges and stomping on cars.
This one likes to inflate like a balloon and float.
And this one flew with bird wings, unnoticed, over skies and ponders
using its talons.

TWO PAINTINGS

1. Girls under Trees

after August Macke

Faces of the faceless.
What does she see now?
Blank and yet perfect.

Where does she go now?
Is there somewhere she can go?
Faces of the faceless.

The other girl,
what does she see?
Blank and yet perfect.

Does she have a face?
Or not?
Faces of the faceless.

Clutch that bag of grain!
It is also full yet clear.
Blank and yet perfect.

Just run, with your
eyes glued to darkness.
Faces of the faceless.
Blank and yet perfect.

2. Girl with Sheep

after Georg Schrimpf

Rise above the ground,
head above the sky,
giantess, hold your sheep.

Yes, lie down on your blanket of moss
and hold your miniature sheep and
rise above the ground.

Look into the baby's eyes,
he is not scared like the others.
Giantess, hold your sheep.

Your island,
floating toward the harbor.
Rise above the ground.

Last hope.
Last chance of joining.
Giantess, hold your sheep.

Let your river skirts flow.
Let your braid sing to the grass.
Rise above the ground,
giantess, hold your sheep.

THE WEIGHT OF THE HEAVENS

Was the Minotaur
really
a monster?

Or was he
just placed here
to scare mankind?

Like Atlas,
who was placed here to live,
instead bearing everything,
the heavens.

What were the heavens like,
I wonder,
and would the Minotaur like it there?

Would it be easier
if you were served by a servant,
who holds you up?

Or would you take pity,
for Atlas already
holds enough?

But how much would the heavens weigh,
if there were
no people?

Does it matter how many people
are there,
for each person adds just a little weight?

Surely the stars weigh more,
or say,
the moon?

And surely the sun burns
Atlas's already weighted
shoulders

or maybe,
the grief
that he isn't out there doing things.

The Minotaur is.

SON OF MAN

after René Magritte

He is the first man, but also the foolish son of man,
he is the ruler, but also the servant,
he is God's flesh, he is a dream.

Adam is walking down the street,
puzzled by all this newness,
puzzled by the picture he sees in a museum,
where it shows him, dressed as he is now—

It must change every day!—with the
apple dangling right in front of his face—
how he wished to taste it again!

He could see Eve, the rib,
just outside the frame, taunting him,
kissing him, the serpent peering from her ear.

So I am me, but also you? he asks the painter.

I am me, and you are you—
you are my invisible father and my child,
the painter replies.

So you are immortal too?

The painter thought and turned
back to Adam, but he was gone—
he was never really there.

A POEM WITH WINGS

This poem
had wings before
being trapped.

This poem was words
ricocheting across the sky
before it was written.

This poem was free
before
it flew through the burning
furnaces of thought.

"Shhh,"
you told the bird
on wings of air.

"Listen,"
you told the bird
perched on your shoulder.

Confinement
in a room
will become your
own little world,
and you will lean
into it,
your soul
will travel and there
will be no more monster,
just a flower,
a walk,
I see the color of your feathers,
I love it so.

Gentle curving of the beak,
the knife-like claws
that scraped
your enemies.

Please become
anew,
be the same,
but different,
my own,
I take you,
I feel you,
I want you,
I write you
down in my little book.

AN ARCHEOLOGY OF THE FUTURE

It will keep on going
and we will be buried,
the ground will take us,
our things,
our shovels will be gone.

And yet,
I stare into the abyss
that I will lie in,
do my work that I know
no one will remember.

I keep myself private,
yet I bring myself joy,
because they had things that we
will never have.

Little doll,
your round,
sweet face,
your limbs have been held
and your dress has been stained.

Moldy pieces of food
that are not ours.
We never open our mouths
or chew.

The only thing we can open is dirt,
dirt is the only thing
we can become.

A small ball
is stuck in time,
its figure deflated,
its body wrinkled like a prune.

I saw a bird's corpse,
and I cradled it.
I found the fox and beat it with a whip.

They are all dead,
and yet,
one is bigger than the other.

When I am dead,
I will shrink to the size of a needle,
to pierce the trees,
I will fall,
I will scream like the ancient owls.

If I found a leaf,
would it rustle elegantly
or would it crumble?

ACKNOWLEDGEMENTS

Thank you to *Stone Soup* for being a space where young people like me can submit their writing and share it with others. *Stone Soup* was where I got my first poem published, and it allowed me to grow as a writer while knowing that my work was being read. Thank you to Caleb Berg for being an amazing blog editor, Conner Bassett for teaching great writing workshops and his encouraging feedback and instruction, Emma Wood for reading everything I submitted and being an awesome editor, William Rubel for founding this exceptional organization, and to everyone else who makes *Stone Soup* work.

And sincere thanks to the editors of the publications where the following poems first appeared:

The Louisville Review: "To You I Grant My Body," "A Poem with Wings"

Rattle Young Poets Anthology: "The Weight of the Heavens"

Stone Soup Magazine: "The Ambassador," "How to Share an Apricot," "Dear Friend," "On an Equestrian Farm [1]," "On an Equestrian Farm [2]," "On a Painting by Henri Rousseau," and "Two Paintings"

Stone Soup Blog: "An Elegy for Bobby Hutton," published as "A Letter: For Bobby Hutton."

ABOUT THE AUTHOR

Emma Catherine Hoff is a writer and poet from New York City, where she lives with her parents and her cat, Gavroche. Her poems have appeared in the *Rattle Young Poets Anthology*, *The Louisville Review*, *The Poetry Society*, and *Stone Soup Magazine*. Her podcast, *Poetry Soup*, as well as book reviews and essays, appear regularly on the Stone Soup Blog. Her poetry collection, *An Archeology of the Future*, won Stone Soup's 2022 Book Contest.

ABOUT STONE SOUP

Founded in 1973, *Stone Soup*—once called "*The New Yorker* of the 8 to 13 set" (*Ms Magazine*)—is the nonprofit literary magazine 100% written and illustrated by kids. We publish a bimonthly print magazine of poetry, fiction, essays, and artwork as well as a blog that includes book reviews, travel diaries, responses to current events, and more—all by kids under fourteen. We also run an annual book contest and have a growing catalog of novels and poetry collections by young writers. The extraordinary writing and art in *Stone Soup* is widely recognized for its excellence, and work from the magazine is routinely included in major school textbooks and assessment tests. You can find more about us at Stonesoup.com or by scanning the QR code at the bottom of this page.

ABOUT THE ANNUAL BOOK CONTEST

Stone Soup has been running an annual book contest since 2020. We publish novels, novellas, and poetry collections by young writers aged fourteen and under. Our submission period runs from March 15 to Aug. 15 each year. To learn more, please visit Stonesoup.com/contests.

PREVIOUS PUBLICATIONS

FICTION
Foxtale by Sarah Hunt (2022)
Born on the First of Two by Anya Geist (2021)
The Other Realm by Tristan Hui (2021)
Three Days till EOC by Abhimanyu Sukhdial (2020)

POETRY
Catalogue of Ripening by Sabrina Guo (2022)
Remember the Flowers by Enni Harlan (2022)
The Golden Elephant by Analise Braddock (2020)
Searching for Bow and Arrows by Tatiana Rebecca Schrayer (2020)

Scan the QR code to visit Stone Soup online:

Printed in the USA
CPSIA information can be obtained
at www.ICGtesting.com
LVHW081923031123
762245LV00050B/9